The Perfect Cocktail

Cookbook

How to Make Unique Cocktails for a Non-Stop Party

BY: Alicia T. White

License Note!

I know you've read this and seen this in many other books and movies. Still, there's a reason why authors and filmmakers are so adamant about protecting their copyrights despite it being so annoying for you to see yet again… The thing is, lots of people infringe on copyrights, and this greatly affects our work negatively.

Thus, here we go again just so things are clear:

Do not make any print or electronic reproductions, sell, re-publish, or distribute this book in parts or as a whole unless you have express written consent from me or my team.

I spent over 4 months working on this cookbook, so I protect it like it's my baby! I know you can understand the value of working hard on something and wanting to protect your end product, so please help me by not infringing on the copyright or letting others do so.

Thanks!

Table of Contents

Introduction:

If you are someone who loves to party and wants to learn how to make delicious cocktails then you're in the right place. Whether you like vodka drinks amazing tequila margaritas or more then read on because you'll learn how to make those and so much more.

Cocktails don't have to be difficult to make and in fact there easy to learn. With this book, you'll be making cocktails like a bartender in no time at all.

ooooooooooooooooooooooooooooooooooooooo

Tequila Drinks

ooooooooooooooooooooooooooooooooooooooo

1. Green Olive Tequila Drink

Cooking Time: 10 minutes

List of Ingredients:

- Coarse salt (option)
- Tequila – 1.5 ounces
- Grand Marnier – 1.5 ounces
- Sweet and sour mix – ½ cup
- Orange juice – 1 ounce
- Crushed ice (as desired)
- Green Olive – 1

OOOOOOOOOOOOOOOOOOOOOOOOOOOOOOOOOOOOOOOOO

Procedure:

A. If you wish to cover the rim of the glass with salt, you can moisten it.

B. Now add the following ingredients to the glass such as sweet and sour mix, tequila, orange juice, and Grand Marnier along with crushed ice.

C. Mix it well and at the end, place the olive on top. Enjoy the drink!

2. Tequila Drink for Fun

Cooking Time: 10 minutes

List of Ingredients:

- Lime – 1
- Coarse Salt – 1 tablespoon
- Jigger tequila – 1.5 fluid ounce
- Lemonade – 5 fluid ounces

OOOOOOOOOOOOOOOOOOOOOOOOOOOOOOOOOOOOOOOOOO

Procedure:

A. Squeeze the lime on the sides of the glass edge from the top and then dip it into the coarse salt.
B. When it is all covered with salt, then add Jigger tequila to the glass with mixing lemonade it.
C. Stir it well and serve!

Cooking Time: 10 minutes

List of Ingredients:

- Ice cubes as desired
- Silver tequila – ½ ounces
- Gin – ½ ounces
- White rum – ½ ounces
- Vodka – ½ ounces
- Triple sec – ½ ounces
- Orange juice – 3 ounces
- Grenadine syrup – 3 ounces
- Beer (any) – 4 ounces

OOOOOOOOOOOOOOOOOOOOOOOOOOOOOOOOOOOOOOOOOOO

Procedure:

A. Get a pitcher and add the following ingredients together such as triple sec, vodka, gin, tequila, rum, grenadine, and orange juice together.

B. Blend it well and then serve it by pouring beer into the glass first and then the blend.

C. Stir it well and then it is ready to serve!

4. Rum Mix Tequila Drink

Cooking Time: 10 minutes

List of Ingredients:

- Ice cubes (as desired)
- Vodka – 1.5 ounces
- Tequila – 1.5 ounces
- Gin – 1.5 ounces
- Blue Curacao – 1.4 ounces
- Sour mix – 1 teaspoon
- Lemon-lime carbonated drink – 2 ounces
- Lemon – 1 slice

OOOOOOOOOOOOOOOOOOOOOOOOOOOOOOOOOOOOOOOO

Procedure:

A. Get a cocktail shaker and add the following ingredients to it such as gin, tequila, vodka, and rum in it. Now add the blue curacao, lemon-lime carbonated drink, and sour mix in it.
B. Shake it well so that all the ingredients blend well.
C. Now pour the drink into the glass and add ice to it. Garnish it with the lemon on the top side of the glass and enjoy the drink!

5. Orange Tequila Drink

Cooking Time: 10 minutes

List of Ingredients:

- Jigger tequila – 1.5 fluid ounce
- Orange juice (fresh) – ¾ cup
- Ice cubes – as desired
- Grenadine syrup – 1.5 fluid ounce
- Orange slice (to garnish) – 1
- Cherry (to garnish) – 1

OOOOOOOOOOOOOOOOOOOOOOOOOOOOOOOOOOOOOOOO

Procedure:

A. Get a glass and add the following ingredients to it such as orange juice, tequila, and grenadine syrup. Mix it well.

B. Add the ice cubes and stir them. In the end, garnish it with an orange slice and cherry on top of the drink to serve!

Vodka & Rum Drinks

6. Raspberry Vodka Drink

Cooking Time: 10 minutes

List of Ingredients:

- Frozen raspberry lemonade concentrate – 1 can
- Vodka – 12 fluid ounces
- Lime – 1

ooooooooooooooooooooooooooooooooooooooo

Procedure:

A. Make the lemonade concentration according to the instructions which are on the can.
B. Now pour it into the glass and add vodka to it.
C. Mix it well and squeeze the lime in it.
D. Stir well, and it is ready to serve!

7. Vodka Coffee Mix Drink

Cooking Time: 10 minutes

List of Ingredients:

- Crushed ice – 1 cup

- Jigger vodka – 1.5 ounce

- Jigger coffee (liqueur) – 1.5 ounce

- Carbonated beverage – 1 can

- Light Cream – 1 ounce

OOOOOOOOOOOOOOOOOOOOOOOOOOOOOOOOOOOOOOOO

Procedure:

A. Add crushed ice into a 16-ounce glass and put vodka along with jigger coffee in it.

B. Now add the carbonated beverage such as cola and mix it well. In the end, pour the light cream on it and blend it well to enjoy the drink.

8. Citron Vodka Drink

Cooking Time: 10 minutes

List of Ingredients:

- Jigger citron vodka – 1.5 ounce
- Blue Curacao – ½ ounce
- Sour mix – 2 ounces
- Lemon-lime carbonated drink – 12 ounces
- Lemon (to garnish) – 1 sliced

OOOOOOOOOOOOOOOOOOOOOOOOOOOOOOOOOOOOOOOO

Procedure:

A. Get a tall glass and add vodka to it.
B. Now add the sour mix along with the blue curacao.
C. Stir it well and then add the lemon carbonated drink to it.
D. Mix it well in the glass and when ready, garnish it with a slice of lemon on the top.

9. Sweet and Sour Vodka Drink

Cooking Time: 10 minutes

List of Ingredients:

- Vodka – 1 ½ ounce
- Sweet and sour mix – 3 ounces
- Carbonated water – 1 cup
- Orange (garnish, slice) – 1
- Cherry (to garnish) – 1
- Ice cubes

oooooooooooooooooooooooooooooooooooooooo

Procedure:

A. Grab a cocktail shaker and add ice to it.
B. Now pour vodka in it along with the sweet and sour mix. Shake it well so both the ingredients are mixed well together.
C. Get a glass and fill it with carbonated water.
D. Now add the mixture to it and then cut the orange slice to place it on the top side of the glass for garnishing. Add the cherry on top with ice according to your desire.

10. Lemon Juice Vodka Drink

Cooking Time: 10 minutes

List of Ingredients:

- Lemon juice – 1 ounce
- Vodka – 2 ounces
- Cranberry juice – 4 ounces
- Ginger ale – 3 ½ ounces

OOOOOOOOOOOOOOOOOOOOOOOOOOOOOOOOOOOOOOOO

Procedure:

A. Get a tall glass and fill it with lemon juice along with vodka. Mix it well with a spoon and then add cranberry juice to it. Pour the ginger ale drink into it and stir it well.
B. When done, it is ready to serve!

Martini Drinks

11. Gin Whiskey Drink

Cooking Time: 5 minutes

List of Ingredients:

- Dry vermouth – 1 ounce
- Gin – 4 ounces
- Green olives – 4

ooooooooooooooooooooooooooooooooooooooooo

Procedure:

A. Get a cocktail shaker and add dry vermouth with gin in it.
B. Shake it well and then serve it in the glass with adding green olives in it.
C. Let it chill and then serve it to enjoy the drink with your friends.

12. Green Olive Martinis

Cooking Time: 10 minutes

List of Ingredients:

- Vodka – 6 ounces
- Vermouth – 1 dash
- Brine (olive jar) – 1 ounce
- Green olives – 4

OOOOOOOOOOOOOOOOOOOOOOOOOOOOOOOOOOOOOOOO

Procedure:

A. Get a glass and mix vermouth and vodka along with brine in it. Stir it well and at the end, add the green olives in it.
B. Enjoy the drink!

13. Orange Flavor Whiskey

Cooking Time: 10 minutes

List of Ingredients:

- White sugar – 2 teaspoons
- Warm water – 2 tablespoons
- Lemon (juiced) – 1
- Vodka – 2 ounces
- Orange Liqueur – 1 ounce
- Ice cubes as needed
- White sugar for rimming

OOOOOOOOOOOOOOOOOOOOOOOOOOOOOOOOOOOOOOOOO

Procedure:

A. Moisten the sides of the glass and rim with white sugar.
B. Pour the following ingredients such as warm water with white sugar, lemon, vodka, and orange liqueur, and mix them well.
C. In the end, add ice cubes as desired and serve!

14. Easy Recipe of Martinis

Cooking Time: 10 minutes

List of Ingredients:

- Vodka – 2 ounces
- Gin – 1 ½ ounces
- Ice cubes as desired
- Lemon peel – 2
- Green olives – 4

OOOOOOOOOOOOOOOOOOOOOOOOOOOOOOOOOOOOOOOO

Procedure:

A. Get a cocktail shaker and add gin and vodka to it. Shake it well and then pour it into a glass.
B. Add the green olives in it and place the lemon peels on top.
C. Serve and enjoy the drink with friends or family.

15. Chocolate Martinis

Cooking Time: 10 minutes

List of Ingredients:

- Chocolate Liqueur – 4 ounces
- Vodka – 2 ounces
- Chocolate (grated) - 1 square

OOOOOOOOOOOOOOOOOOOOOOOOOOOOOOOOOOOOOOO

Procedure:

A. Get a cocktail mixer and add vodka and chocolate liqueur to it.
B. Shake it well, and then pour it into a glass. At the top of it, garnish it with grated chocolate.

Margarita Drinks

OOOOOOOOOOOOOOOOOOOOOOOOOOOOOOOOOOOO

16. Frozen Limeade Margarita

Cooking Time: 10 minutes

List of Ingredients:

- Gold tequila – 1.5 ounces
- Triple sec – 1.5 ounces
- Frozen limeade concentrate – 12 ounces
- Ice as desired

ooooooooooooooooooooooooooooooooooooooo

Procedure:

A. Grab a blender and mix the ingredients in it such as triple sec, limeade concentrate, and triple sec in it.
B. Blend it well and when ready, serve it in a glass with desired ice cubes in it.

17. Pineapple Margarita Drink

Cooking Time: 10 minutes

List of Ingredients:

- Pineapple juice – ½ cup
- Orange juice – ½ cup
- Lemonade (concentrated) – 2 cups
- Tequila – 2 ounces
- Orange liqueur – 1 ounce

OOOOOOOOOOOOOOOOOOOOOOOOOOOOOOOOOOOOOOOO

Procedure:

A. Get a glass of your choice and add the following ingredients to it such as orange juice, pineapple juice, and lemonade along with tequila in it.
B. Mix it well and then add the orange liqueur.
C. Stir it and then enjoy it with your friends and family.

18. Simple Margarita with Tequila

Cooking Time: 10 minutes

List of Ingredients:

- Lime juice – 1 ¼ cup
- Triple sec – 1 cup
- Tequila – 1 cup
- Fresh lemon juice – 3 tablespoons
- Ice cubes as desired

OOOOOOOOOOOOOOOOOOOOOOOOOOOOOOOOOOOOOOOOO

Procedure:

A. Get a blender and add the following ingredients to it such as fresh lemon juice, tequila, lime juice, and triple sec.
B. Blend it well and when ready, serve it with desired ice cubes by pouring it into a glass.

19. Pomegranate Margarita Drink

Cooking Time: 10 minutes

List of Ingredients:

- Tequila – 1 cup
- Triple sec – 1 cup
- Confectioners' sugar – ¼ cup
- Ice as desired
- Lime juice – 1 cup
- Pomegranate juice – 1 cup

OOOOOOOOOOOOOOOOOOOOOOOOOOOOOOOOOOOOOOO

Procedure:

A. Get a pitcher and add the triple sec and tequila in it.
B. Mix it well and then add sugar to it. Now mix it until the sugar gets dissolved in it.
C. Add the pomegranate juice in it with lime juice.
D. Mix it well and then serve the drink in a glass.

Cooking Time: 10 minutes

List of Ingredients:

- Coconut cream – 1 can
- Ice cubes as desired
- Tequila – ¾ cup
- Lime juice (fresh) – ½ cup
- Orange liqueur – ¼ cup

OOOOOOOOOOOOOOOOOOOOOOOOOOOOOOOOOOOOOOOO

Procedure:

A. Get a blender and add the following ingredients to it such as coconut cream, tequila, lime juice, and orange liqueur.
B. Blend it well and then add desired ice cubes in it to serve!

21. Lime Margarita Drink

Cooking Time: 10 minutes

List of Ingredients:

- Sugar – 2/3 cup
- Water – 1/3 cup
- Lemon juice (fresh) – 1 ½ cups
- Egg white – 1
- Ice cubes as desired
- Tequila – 2 cups
- Cointreau – 1 cup
- Lime juice – ½ cup
- Lime wedges – 16
- Salt for the rim of a glass
- Sugar – ¼ cup
- Water – 2 ¼ cups

OOOOOOOOOOOOOOOOOOOOOOOOOOOOOOOOOOOOOOOOO

Procedure:

A. First of all, mix the sugar (2/3 cup) and water (1/3 cup) with boiling it well. When boiled, keep it on the side to cool.

B. On the other side, stir the water (2 ¼ cups), sugar (1/4 cup), egg white, and lemon juice together. Mix it well so it becomes like a sour mix.

C. Get a pitcher and add the following ingredients to it such as tequila, lime juice, Cointreau, syrup of sugar and water as well as the sour mix. Blend it well and then add ice to it as desired.

D. Coat the rims of the glass with salt and pour the drink into it to serve!

22. Grapefruit Margarita Drink

Cooking Time: 10 minutes

List of Ingredients:

- Ice cubes as desired
- Tequila – 2 ounces
- Orange Liqueur – 1 ounce
- Lime juice – 1 ounce
- Grapefruit Soda – 2 ounces

OOOOOOOOOOOOOOOOOOOOOOOOOOOOOOOOOOOOOO

Procedure:

A. Get a glass and pour the following ingredients in it such as lime juice, tequila, and orange liqueur along with grapefruit soda.
B. Mix it well and serve it with desired ice cubes in it.

23. Orange Margarita Drink

Cooking Time: 10 minutes

List of Ingredients:

- Orange liqueur – 2 ounces
- Tequila – 2 ounces
- Lime juice – 1 ounce
- Agave Nectar – 1 ounce

ooooooooooooooooooooooooooooooooooooooooo

Procedure:

A. Get a glass of your choice and add the following ingredients to it such as tequila, orange liqueur, lime juice, and agave nectar.

B. Mix it well and then it is ready to serve!

24. Lemon Tequila Mix Margarita

Cooking Time: 10 minutes

List of Ingredients:

- Lime juice – 1
- Lemon – ½ slice
- White sugar – 2 tablespoons
- Tequila – 2 ounces
- Ice cubes as desired
- Orange liqueur to taste
- Salt – 1 tablespoon

ooooooooooooooooooooooooooooooooooooooooo

Procedure:

A. Moisten the rim of the glass with lime juice and dip it in the salt for it to cover the rims. Add tequila to the glass with sugar in it and mix it well.
B. Now add orange liqueur in it as desired with ice cubes. In the end, garnish it with the lemon on the top side of the glass and serve!

25. Banana Flavor Margarita

Cooking Time: 10 minutes

List of Ingredients:

- Lemon juice – 2 tablespoons
- Lime juice – 2 tablespoons
- Banana liqueur – ¾ cup
- Tequila – ½ cup
- Triple sec – ¼ cup
- Ice cubes as desired
- Bananas – 2

OOOOOOOOOOOOOOOOOOOOOOOOOOOOOOOOOOOOOOO

Procedure:

A. Get a blender and add the following ingredients to it such as tequila, lemon juice, lime juice, bananas, triple sec, and banana liqueur in it.
B. Blend it well and when the texture is thick, pour it into a glass to serve by adding ice in it as desired.

Whiskey Drinks

26. Pineapple Whiskey Drink

Cooking Time: 10 minutes

List of Ingredients:

- Orange juice (concentrated) – 6 ounces
- Lemonade (concentrated) – 12 ounces
- Pineapple juice – 1 can
- White sugar – 1 ½ cups
- Brewed black tea – 2 cups
- Whiskey – 2 cups
- Lemon-lime carbonated beverage – 1 bottle

OOOOOOOOOOOOOOOOOOOOOOOOOOOOOOOOOOOOOOOO

Procedure:

A. Get a pitcher and add the following ingredients to it such as orange juice, lemonade, pineapple juice, white sugar, and whiskey. Mix it well.
B. Then add brewed black tea along with a lemon-lime carbonated beverage. Stir it well and then pour it into a glass to serve.

27. Whiskey Clove Drink

Cooking Time: 10 minutes

List of Ingredients:

- Cloves – 8
- Lemon slice – 1
- White sugar – 1 tablespoon
- Water (boiled) – ¾ cup
- Irish whiskey – 1.5 ounces

OOOOOOOOOOOOOOOOOOOOOOOOOOOOOOOOOOOOOOOO

Procedure:

A. Get a lemon slice and press the cloves into it all around.
B. Now grab a glass and add the following ingredients to it such as boiled water and sugar.
C. Mix it well and when the sugar is mixed properly then add Irish whiskey to it.
D. Now when it is mixed, place the lemon slice on it, and it is ready to serve when chilled.

28. Cinnamon Whiskey Drink

Cooking Time: 10 minutes

List of Ingredients:

- Honey – 1 teaspoon
- Water (boiled) – 2 ounces
- Whiskey – 1 ½ ounces
- Cloves – 3
- Cinnamon stick – 1
- Lemon (sliced) – 1
- Nutmeg – a pinch

ooooooooooooooooooooooooooooooooooooooooo

Procedure:

A. Get a mug and add the following ingredients to it such as whiskey, honey, and boiling water.
B. Stir it well and then add the cinnamon stick with cloves in it.
C. Now let the mixture settle and then put the lemon slice off the top of it to enjoy the drink!

29. Scotch Whiskey Drink

Cooking Time: 1o minutes

List of Ingredients:

- Scotch whiskey – ¼ cup
- Sweet vermouth – 2 tablespoons
- Ice cubes as desired
- Angostura bitters – 2 dashes
- Cherry to garnish – 1

OOOOOOOOOOOOOOOOOOOOOOOOOOOOOOOOOOOOOOO

Procedure:

A. Get a glass and add vermouth and scotch whiskey to it.

B. Mix it well and then add the Angostura bitters in it. Stir it well and add ice cubes.

C. When ready to serve, put the cherry on the drink to enjoy it!

30. Cherries Whiskey Drink

Cooking Time: 10 minutes

List of Ingredients:

- Orange juice (concentrated) – 12 ounces
- Lemonade (concentrated) – 12 ounces
- Water – 18 cups
- Whiskey – 2 cups
- Cherries (to garnish) – 2
- Orange slices – 2

OOOOOOOOOOOOOOOOOOOOOOOOOOOOOOOOOOOOOOOO

Procedure:

A. Get a pitcher and add the following ingredients in it such as water, whiskey, orange juice, and lemon juice.
B. Stir it well and then pour it into the glass when you have to serve.
C. Place the cherries and orange slices on the glass when you are about to serve.

Author's Note

Not many people do this, but I grew up under difficult circumstances where nothing was handed to me, and the only way forward was with your best effort. At some point, people started recognizing me for my talent in the kitchen despite my young age, and I've only worked harder from there!

Because I am constantly trying to improve my work, I would really appreciate your help. Sure, I always ask my friends and family for their feedback on my newest projects but, whether they want to accept it or not, there's always some sort of bias because they don't want to hurt my feelings by criticizing my work. Thus, I need a neutral pair of eyes — that's where you come in!

If you're up for it, I would appreciate you telling me what you think of my cookbooks. Are the recipes easy to follow? Did you get stuck somewhere? Are the measurements laid out? Any suggestions you may have are welcome. After all, cookbooks are only helpful when you actually understand them! Incorporating your ideas and suggestions into my new projects will be my show of eternal gratitude because you can only be the best at something by constantly improving and being open to change.

Thanks!

Alicia T. White

About the Author

Alicia had a tough childhood and had to take care of her siblings early. Although they often helped her with making the beds and washing, Alicia was responsible for cooking since she was the oldest of six. Being in the kitchen was still very difficult at her age, but she learned her way around the stove and oven throughout the years.

Whereas her first dishes were practically inedible, burnt rice and mushy pasta… Eventually, she turned to the oven for help as many of the dishes she wanted to make were too complicated. Nonetheless, her baked casseroles were amazing! Most importantly, they were simple and required way less clean-up.

At first, they were simple pasta bakes, but once Alicia got the hang of things, she was baking all sorts of meals. When it came to spreading the word of her delicious cooking, having 5 siblings was extremely advantageous. Soon, neighbors were placing orders for some of her casseroles! Eventually, Alicia was doing so well with the business that she hired extra help. Now it's one of the most affordable yet popular weeknight casserole services in the mid-West!

Today, she still lives with her siblings and is working hard to teach them about the family business that led them out of poverty. She likes to publish cookbooks on casseroles and one-pot meals in her free time— basically anything quick and easy. Her motto is, "If a seven-year-old can't make it, it isn't simple enough!"

9 798366 253741